Pop-Up and 3-D Cards

Step-by-Step Projects to Make at Home

Emma Angel

COLLINS & BROWN

Produced in 2004 by
PRC Publishing Limited
The Chrysalis Building
Bramley Road, London W10 6SP
An imprint of Chrysalis Books Group

First published in Great Britain in 2004 by
Collins & Brown
The Chrysalis Building
Bramley Road, London W10 6SP
An imprint of Chrysalis Books Group

1 2 3 4 5 6 7 8 9

ISBN: 1-84340-228-9

Printed in Malaysia

Acknowledgements:

A big "thank you" to the following people who helped during
the making of this book:
Simon Clay for the fabulous photographs. Jo Pink and Hettie
for assisting with the styling. Rachael Moore for the pop-up
pouches, technical help and moral support. Caroline Bartl for
being a card-making guru. Mario Forzan for the cooking and
for keeping me sane. Lucy Clink for being my best friend.
Katherine Gilhooley for being my mum, without whom none
of this would be possible, and Jon Clawley for putting up with
me and my paper obsession!

Picture Credits:

All photographs © Chrysalis Image Library / Simon Clay.

Contents

Introduction

This book takes you on a voyage into the exciting world of three-dimensional or 3-D cards. If you've ever found yourself bored with sending yet another flat and lifeless card, this book will help you to find a new dimension to the cards you make and send to people. Making cards can be a very rewarding hobby, not only pleasing to the crafter but pleasing to the recipient too. There are so many possibilities to explore once we step outside of the standard 2-D card techniques: layering, cutting, pop-ups, foldouts, and concertinas. Let your imagination go. The techniques are a lot of fun to master as well.

This guide contains 18 card projects and four envelope projects, one of which is a pop-up pouch envelope. Included are ideas for developing projects and for variations on themes. This book is stuffed full of card-making ideas. All seasonal occasions are covered – you will never have to buy a mass-produced card again! Projects can be adapted and altered to personal taste or to commemorate particular events.

Everybody who is interested in cards and paper craft will be able to use this book, young and old alike. Most young children regularly read pop-up books and wonder how they are made. Now they can find out, as the early projects are easy enough for children to make. Even the simplest of pop-ups can look dramatic!

What is a Pop-up Card?

A pop-up card contains an illustration that is activated either by opening the card or by lifting a flap. This movement makes the image become 3-D. Used in this way, paper becomes an inspirational medium and can be used to dramatic effect. Ingenious constructions seem to almost make the paper come to life. This book contains techniques that will enable you to make flying mechanisms, animated mouths, spinning wheels that allow colours to change, tabs that when pulled allow movement, pop-up boxes, open-up flaps, concertinas, springs and 3-D tunnels.

Pop-up History

In the UK in the 18th century (before TV and computer games) "novelty books" were created to amuse readers. The first of these was the "Harlequinade," by Robert Sayer in 1765. Based on pantomimes and the trouble-causing caricature Harlequin, it had moveable pictures, which delighted children and adults alike.

The second half of the 19th century was a boom period for the pop-up book. Technology advanced in die-cutting and printing, and the craftsmanship of these books improved. Their creators became more like paper engineers.

In Germany, "dissolving" picture books were produced. Tabs could be pulled, allowing scenes to change. One of the most famous pop-up paper engineers was Lothar Meggendorfer (1847–1925) from Munich. He is credited with inventing pull-tabs, which were used to animate books.

While pop-up books became successful, greeting cards were also gaining popularity. Henry Cole is credited with

inventing the first Christmas card in 1843. The coming of the Victorian age led to the principles of pop-up books being applied to cards as well. By the late Victorian era, "trick cards" had come into being. Cards became almost like mechanical toys. The ingenuity of the Victorian age meant that die-cutting and embossing cards became very complex yet remained delicate. Soldiers kicked their legs; doors opened to reveal Christmas scenes inside houses and figures in nativity scenes stood up.

The term "pop-up" was not used until the early 1930s when the Blue Ribbon Press of Chicago copyrighted it. They mass-produced pop-up books of cartoon characters, such as Walt Disney's "Mickey Mouse".

Paper engineers are still continuing to delight us. Following on from the same traditions and working alongside graphic designers, they now produce all manner of pop-up cards, calendars, paper toys, books, flyers, brochures, leaflets and invitations. They are still exploring the versatility and tactile qualities of paper.

How to Use This Book

Each project has step-by-step photos and instructions to guide you. Some projects have templates at the back of the book that you will need to enlarge using a photocopier and trace. There are "You Will Need" sections at the start of each project that will let you know what materials to gather together. Most of the projects require A4-size card unless other sizes are mentioned. All of the projects require a glue stick and scissors, unless otherwise stated. The illustrated techniques are only suggestions, so feel free to alter them. Each project offers ideas for developing the final card or other cards you could make by using the same suggested principle. Also included are suggestions for making decorative envelopes. Envelope templates are at the end of the book for you to use too.

Children also will want to get in on the action. They love making pop-up cards, as do young-at-heart adults. Young children should use safety scissors rather than sharp scissors. Any cutting with a craft knife will have to be done by an adult, as will any gluing with strong glue. Projects such as Fab Fairy Card, Springy Garden Card, Cracking Easter Card and Happy House Card are particularly suitable for kids to make under adult supervision.

You may already have an idea for a pop-up card, in which case you can decide which project is closest to your idea. There is plenty of room for your own interpretation. You might think about who is going to receive the card and their likes and dislikes. The best thing about making a card is personalising it to fit the individual who will receive it. Try to think about what they like, what colours they often wear, what colours the interior of their house is painted in. Do they collect anything? Have they got a passion for pigs, pearl earrings or chocolate cake?

Alternatively, just let your imagination run wild. Be proud of your creations. Be warned though, you may not want to give them away. If you wish to begin but don't know where to start, just pick something that looks as if it might be fun!

Getting Started

Paper

How is Paper Made?

Paper can be made by hand or machine. Differently woven machine-made paper has fibres that tend to run in one direction, while they are random in handmade paper.

Paper can be described as a thin sheet of pulped fibres. It is generally made from wood fibres and the principle for making it has changed little in 2000 years. Cellulose fibres are beaten, soaked in water and sieved to form a wet pulp. Papermaking machines have a continuously moving wire belt onto which wet pulp is poured. As the wire moves, the water is drained off and pressed out; this helps to dry the paper.

Choosing Paper and Card

Paper can be a very inspirational medium in itself. Texture and colour are the main qualities. Colours can be combined to look playful and fun or subtle and serious. When choosing paper, imagine what kind of final card you want to create. Think about the recipient's favourite colours or colours associated with particular events or festivities, such as Christmas.

The varieties of paper available can be somewhat overwhelming, as there are, quite simply, thousands of different types to choose from. I have chosen just a few to use in this book that should be easy to find in most specialist paper stores or art shops.

Types of Paper

Plain paper and **card** are made from wood pulp for a smooth texture. They are a great staple for the card maker and are avaliable in a kaleidoscopic range of colours.

Coated card, such as **metallic**, **mirrored** and **pearlescent** types of card, are made from plain card that has been finished with a varnish to give a glossy or metallic appearance. They can look luxuriant, futuristic or high-tech.

Printed card, such as **wood-effect**, **holographic** and **animal print** are plain papers that have been printed before being varnished. They can be used to add interest to projects. If you can't find the right type of printed card in an art shop make your own by gluing a colour copy to a sheet of card to strengthen it.

Laid, **texture** or **corrugated card** are plain papers that have been textured by embossing or debossing with metal plates. Corrugated card has a ribbed surface that makes it sturdy and protective. Its texture shouldn't make it any more difficult to cut, score and fold.

Opaque papers are similar to tracing papers in opacity and weight. They can be brightly coloured yet still have a translucent quality.

Newspapers, **old magazines**, **colour copies** and **photocopies** are useful for collage purposes. Thin printed paper can also be used to make interesting envelopes. Easy to get hold of and inexpensive.

Wrapping paper is generally thin, which makes it ideal for collaging; a great way to add splashes of colour or pattern to a card. Paper can be bought by the sheet or in cost-effective rolls. Stick two sheets together to thicken it.

Wallpaper is useful as a craft material due to colour and texture. It is strong and durable, easy to cut, fold and glue. A cheap but unusual material to use for card crafting, you could look for old rolls of wallpaper in the attic or at boot fairs.

Handmade paper is rarely smooth but is textured due to the lumpier nature of the pulp from which it is made. It is often imbedded with petals, seeds, metallic papers, sequins or threads. It is better to use it for decorative purposes for pop-up cards, as it doesn't score or fold well.

Paper Sizes and Weight

- A3 (29.7 x 42cm) is half A2.
- A4 (21x 29.7cm) is half A3. This is the standard size for an international business letter.
- A5 (14.8 x 21cm) is half A4. When folded in half, it makes the perfect size for a greeting card.

Most card can be bought in A3 and A4-sized sheets. These are useful sizes, as there is no wastage when making cards. They are portable sizes too. It can be difficult to carry large sheets of paper that have not been rolled without damaging them.

Card needn't be heavy or thick to make pop-up cards; 170gsm should be enough.

Paper Storage

It is a good idea to store paper flat. Keeping it rolled up damages the fibres. To stop edges from curling, keep it somewhere that is non humid. Store it in an artist's portfolio or keep it flat under your bed, sandwiched between two sheets of thick card. Keep it away from feet that could kick or knock the edges.

Testing the Grain

Machine-made paper is made from plant fibres and can be described as having a grain not unlike cloth. The technical term for this is the "run" of the paper. To find which way the paper "runs", hold the paper by two different edges and see if it bends more from one edge than the other. If it bends more one way, then that is the direction of the fibres and the "run".

Equipment

If you are a regular paper crafter, you will most probably have the following tools. Anything you are missing can be found in a good art shop:

- Rulers – metal (for use with a knife) and plastic
- Cutting tools – craft knife and cutting mat, scissors, wavy-edged scissors
- Pencils – retractable pencils are a great tool for precision marking with erasers
- Glues – craft glue, glue sticks, strong adhesives, double-sided tape, one-sided tape, fixer pads
- Tracing paper

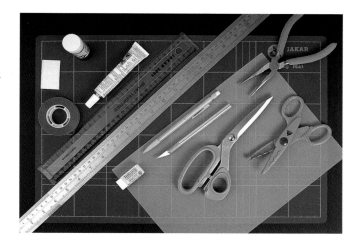

Art Materials

You may already have a good collection of art materials built up from doing different craft projects. If you haven't got everything, don't worry. Start with whatever materials you have available.

- Coloured inks
- Black ink and stamp pad
- Spray paints
- Felt-tip pens
- Fine liner pens
- Wax crayons
- Pencil crayons
- A basic set of acrylic paints
- Palette
- Paintbrushes in a mixture of small and medium sizes

Embellishments

Finding embellishments to use with paper is a fun hobby in itself. Try to source materials that are fairly flat, such as sequins, stickers, and ribbons. Store them separately in divided plastic holders, art boxes, jam jars or labelled envelopes. That way you won't have to spend hours searching for each tiny trimming. Some embellishments can be found around the house. For others, you may need to go to a haberdashery or a specialist art or craft shop.

Items, such as craft punches, can be purchased fairly cheaply and are worth collecting. They can be used to punch shapes from single sheets of paper. Punches are easy to use and don't wear out for years. In addition, they come in hundreds of different shapes and sizes and produce sharp, accurate shapes.

Glitter glues and glittery fabric paints are handy to keep in your art box. They provide a quick way to add a touch of glitter to a finished card without the mess of loose glitter. Sealing wax and initial seals can be bought from specialist stationers.

Not only are they attractive items in themselves, but they can be used to seal envelopes in a unique way.

Collect trimmings that will inspire you at a later date. How about looking in unusual places? You could try fabric shops, markets or even charity shops.

- Sequins – with and without holes
- Strings of sequins
- Thin and thick ribbons
- Stickers – stars and hearts
- Fabric flowers in different colours and sizes
- Wiggly eyes in a mixture of sizes
- Brass split pins
- Silver earring wires
- Silver jewellery posts
- Glitter glues
- Fabric paint
- Daisy craft punch
- Butterfly craft punch
- Single-hole punch
- Silver sealing wax and safety lighter
- Initial seals
- Coloured, holographic, fluorescent and clear sticky tapes
- Household wire

Basic Techniques and Safety Advice

Scoring and Making a Card Blank

Scoring needs to be crisp and accurate for successful pop-ups. You can score a fold line either by grazing the surface of the paper with a craft knife and a steel ruler or by making a dent with a blunt object such as a knitting needle and a ruler. This will compress the fibres and make it easier to flex. If you are using a knife, be careful to graze the surface rather than cutting clean through.

Score and fold parallel to the paper grain. Make the score on the inside of the fold, because scoring often produces an embossed ridge.

To make a card blank, cut the card to the appropriate size. Then mark the centre of the card and score lengthways with a metal ruler and knife.

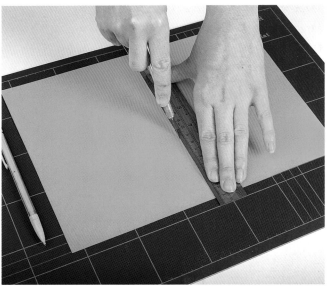

Cutting

Equipment, such as scissors, a craft knife and cutting mat are essential tools for card crafters. A steel ruler will allow you to cut card accurately. If you use a plastic ruler, you will invariably cut the edge of the ruler, rather than the card!

The cutting mat will save the table underneath from getting scratched and cut. A little practice is needed when cutting shapes with a knife. Curves require a firm, swift motion. It is best to cut things all in one go rather than to stop and start – this can create a jagged edge. Follow a pencil line and press down hard to get the most accurate cut.

Folding

There are two types of folds. One sticks upward like the peak of a mountain, the other dips downward like a valley. These step-by-step photos will show you which type of fold to use in each case. Fold lines are indicated on templates by a dotted line. Cuts are represented with a straight line.

Folding without the aid of scoring will damage the fibres in a card and can cause cracking or splintering, which can make your card look unprofessional. Once your card has been scored, fold it over and rub over the spine (outside of the fold) with a rounded object, such as a jar. Always fold on a flat surface free from clutter, so as to avoid making dents in your card.

Transferring an Image

The templates at the back of this book can be enlarged by using a photocopier to make them the correct size. The percentage they need to be enlarged to is given. Once you have enlarged a template, you can trace it. To trace an image, you will need to use tracing paper and a pencil. Lay paper over the top of an image and copy the edge with a pencil. Then flip the tracing paper over and retrace the line on the back.

Turn the tracing paper over again and lay it on the paper or card you wish to use for the final piece. Retrace around the original pencil line and the image will be reproduced neatly.

Illustrating Your Cards

Before illustrating your cards, it is a good idea to try mock-ups with plain white card. Check that your pop-up card really works well before spending too much time decorating it.

Some of the projects in this book contain elements of one or two of the following techniques. Using a mixture of colouring media makes the finished card more interesting. Use an explosion of colour on your pop-up card if you are using plain card. Keep the decoration to a minimum if you are using patterned, mirrored or handmade paper.

Collage: Magazines, newspapers, wrapping paper, wallpaper, handmade paper, photocopies, colour copies, decoupage scraps and stickers could all be used to make interesting collages. Cut out images you like as you find them and save them in envelopes for later use. Collage is a quick and effective way to decorate your card. It does not require any drawing that can go wrong or messy painting, or any need to wait for paint, inks or glitter glues to dry. Collage can therefore sometimes be advantageous, especially if you are in a rush to get a card posted to arrive in time.

Pens and Pencils: It is a good idea to collect a mixture of different coloured pencil crayons and fibre-tipped pens. Look for pens of varying thicknesses too. Drawing outlines with black fine liners will create a cartoon-style image. Colour them in with pencils and felt-tips for no fuss illustrations. Pencils can be used to add shading or highlights to pre-painted areas as well. For this, it is worth investing in a good pencil sharpener or a craft knife.

Painting: Acrylic paints are fast drying and can be mixed to create precise colours. A basic set of white, black, brown, green, blue, red and yellow paints has been used to mix all of the colours used in this book. A light pink colour can be created from a mixture of white, red and yellow paints. You will need to use mostly white, with just a dash of red and yellow. Bold colours can be turned into pastels by mixing them with white. Adding black to pastel colours will just muddy them. As acrylics dry quickly, you will need to mix and use them straight away. If you have mixed too much of a colour and want to save it for another time, use sealable plastic pots. A suitable container is the small screw-top pots you can often buy in chemists to hold toiletries when travelling. Don't forget to wash brushes with soapy water as soon as you have used them. Once acrylic has dried onto the bristles, to remove it is very difficult, if not impossible.

Foam Prints: Thin foam used with an inked stamp pad can be used to repeat images. This is like a more refined version of the potato print. Draw a design on the foam with a ball point pen, cut it out and glue to an old jar or lid. Ink it and press down firmly onto the card. Only the raised foam image will be transferred. You can also use a ballpoint pen to make dents in the foam. Any dents will result in a gap in the ink on the finished piece.

Craft spray paints can be used to add quick bursts of colour to cards or use them with a stencil to repeat designs. They are available in lots of different colours as well as metallic. Buy them from craft shops and DIY stores; they work out to be cost-effective as a little paint goes a long way. Wash the nozzles after use to stop them from becoming blocked with dried paint. Store them upright and keep them out of the reach of children.

Wax Resistant Effects: Wax crayons and ink (or watercolour paint) can be used to create interesting effects. Draw with the crayon and then paint over it. The ink or paint will be unable to cling to the wax. Only the areas without wax can be coloured by the paint creating a mottled effect.

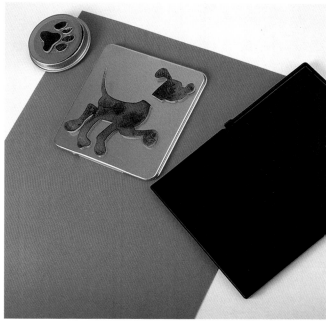

Safety Advice

Card crafting isn't a dangerous hobby, but there are always safety issues to consider. Be careful when cutting with a craft knife. It is easy to slip the knife away from the paper, especially when applying lots of pressure. This could not only ruin your creation, but cause injury to yourself. Always use a cutting mat to protect your table. Craft knives, any glue stronger than a glue stick, sharp scissors and spray paints should be kept away from young children.

If you are planning to spray paint for the Valentine Hearts Card, it is a good idea to spray on newspaper or inside an old cardboard box. This will stop the paint from spreading to floors or walls.

Envelopes

If you are going to post your cards, you could make matching envelopes. There are templates at the end of this book for the straight-edged envelope, v-flap envelope and pop-up pouch. The origami envelope is made purely by folding. In all cases, you will want the front of the envelope to be slightly bigger than card by about 1cm.

If you don't have time to make envelopes, buy manufactured ones to the sizes suggested. For envelope sizes, see C-sizes in the Glossary. You could try jollying up shop bought envelopes by decorating them to match the card.

Origami Envelope

You could try experimenting with lots of different papers, such as pages from magazines, wrapping paper or hand-decorated papers. I've used spray-painted paper, and nail varnish splashed paper. Try using unusual methods to secure the flaps of the envelope – I've tried a badge and wiggly eyes – or how about plasters for a "get well soon" card!

If you've used a patterned paper, use a white oblong label on the front of the envelope for the address.

How to Make It

You will need an A4 sheet of paper to make an envelope for a folded A5 card. An A4 sheet will also make an envelope for a postcard. An A3 sheet will be needed to make an envelope for a folded A4 card. To secure the flap of the envelope, you will also need, glue, stickers, tape or sealing wax.

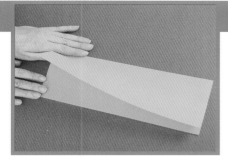

1 Fold the sheet of paper in half lengthways.

2 Open out flat and fold the top corners of the paper to the middle fold line. This will look like the triangular roof on top of a house.

3 Lay the card close to the triangles, making sure it is central.

4 Fold one side inwards over the cards.

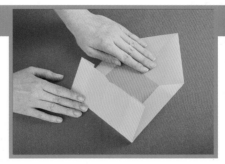

5 Fold in the other side and fold the bottom piece over the card.

6 Fold the flap over the card and stick it down with glue, stickers or tape.

Straight-edged Envelope

You could try using newsprint, black paper, marbled paper, metallic paper or photocopied paper to create unusual envelopes. Have a go at sealing the flap using silver wax; it looks great with black.

This envelope can be scaled to fit any size of card. Just change the measurements.

How to Make It

You will need an A4 sheet of paper or larger, depending on your finished card, scissors, ruler, glue or double-sided tape. To close the envelope, use glue, tape, stickers or wax and a seal.

1   Copy the template at the back of the book onto a piece of paper.

2   Cut out the envelope shape.

3   fold the bottom inwards using a ruler as a guide.

4   Fold the sides inwards.

5   Glue the sides with a glue stick.

6   Seal the flap with melted sealing wax by lighting the wick with a safety lighter. Allow the wax to melt and drip it onto the flap. You can then press the hot wax with a seal.

V-flap Envelope

This envelope needn't be a square; you can alter the measurement to make it into an oblong if you prefer. You could line the inside of this envelope with wrapping paper to create a two-toned envelope or try hand-decorated spotty paper. You could try drawing lines on the front of the envelope with a glitter pen or paints. Try using a melted wax crayon as sealing wax. Use funky coloured tape or stickers to secure the flap.

Follow the instructions as with the previous envelope. Use the template at the back of this book.

Pop-up Pouch

This pop-up pouch is a novel way to post greeting cards. If the finished card is raised or 3-D, you can rest assured it won't get squashed when posted, especially if you use a heavy weight card to make the pouch. When you are assembling the pop-up pouch, it appears to be flat, push the side flaps inwards and up it pops.

Copy the template at the back of the book onto card. Score along the dotted lines and cut it out along the solid black line. Use strong glue or double-sided tape to stick the tab to the underside of the card. Fold the flaps inwards. If posting, stuff the pouch with shredded paper and glue the flaps shut. You could decorate it with glitter glue or puffy paint to mark out lines where the address could go. You could also use an address label, scrap of card, or a playing card on which to write the address.

V-fold Cards
Hollywood Cocktail Card

Congratulations or Happy Anniversary

The inspiration for these cards comes from Hollywood screen sirens and the cocktails they sipped. Since cocktails have a reputation for sophisticated celebrations these would make great congratulations, engagement or anniversary cards. The image, taken from a vintage magazine is used for an elegant and glamorous look. It has been applied to silver card to give the illusion that a reflection has just been caught in the glass. The colour scheme of dusky pink, grey and silver evokes a nostalgic feel. The pearlescent finishing on the card looks retro too. Sequins and stars on the base of the card add a hint of Hollywood glitz.

    To make this card appeal to men as well, you could keep the cocktail theme but make it more masculine by creating a pop-up cocktail shaker from silver card. You could try writing cocktail recipes on the base of the card too. Mine's a martini, shaken not stirred. The cocktail is constructed from a simple v-fold. It is a "double page pop-up" as the base sits on both sides of the opened out card allowing it to pop-up when the card is opened. There is a template of the cocktail glass at the back of the book for you to use.

You Will Need

- A3 pink pearlescent card
- Grey pencil
- Silver card
- Ruler
- Scissors
- Craft knife
- White acrylic paint
- Fine paintbrush
- 2 colour-copied images from a vintage magazine
- Glue stick
- Pink glitter glue
- Sequins
- Sticky tape
- Pink bendy straw

1   Start by making a card blank with the pink pearlescent card, 11cm x 30cm, then score and fold it in half.

2   Draw stars on the pearly side of the card blank with a grey pencil.

3   Draw a cocktail shape on silver card (see template at the back of book). Draw a line down the centre of the cocktail shape with a ruler.

7   Glue the triangular image to the cocktail with a glue stick.

8   Edge the rim of the glass with pink glitter glue. Edge the inside of the card with pink glitter. You may need to practice piping the glitter first on a scrap of card.

9   When the glitter is dry, glue the tabs of the cocktail to the card. Make sure that the crease in the card and glass match up. The tabs should be placed an equal distance from either side of the crease to make sure the card will fold correctly.

Other Cocktail Cards

Cherry Cocktail

Repeat steps 1–4 and 7–9. To decorate the cocktail:

1   Paint a star and colour in the stem with dark purple paint.

2   Paint a cherry with red paint.

3   Paint the liquid part of the cocktail with gold glitter.

4   Edge the rim of the glass with pink glitter.

5   Tape on a thin strip of black card for the cocktail stick.

Bubbly Cocktail

Decorate the cocktail with bubbles or circles cut from leftover pearlescent card. Decorate the card with circles of silver card and leftover scraps from the colour copy of the magazine. Make a lemon from a semi-circle of silver card, paint it with yellow and white acrylic paints and glue it to the cocktail. Paint on highlights and stars in white acrylic.

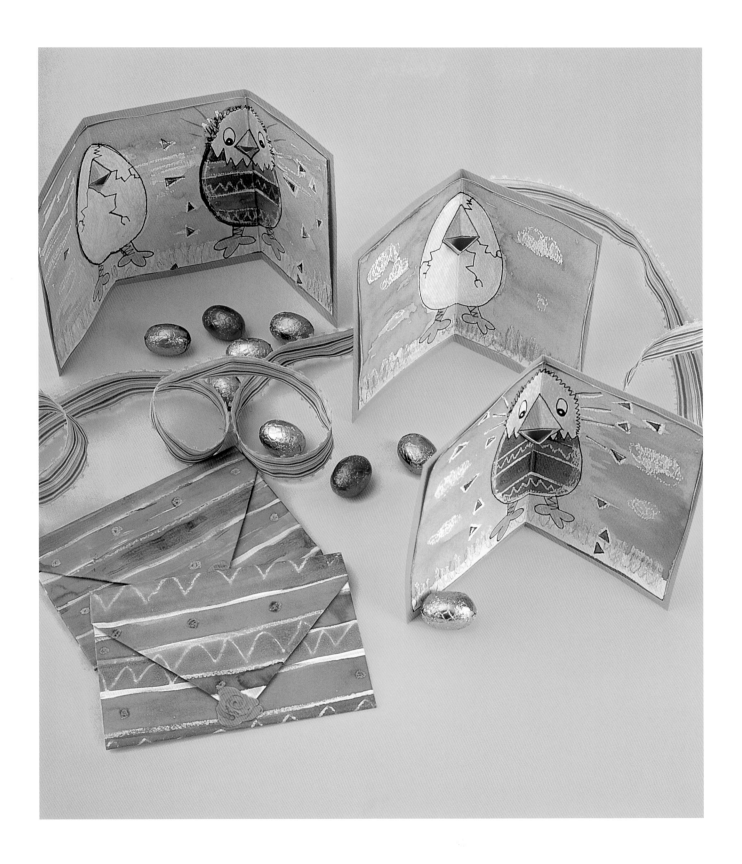

1   Make a cream card blank, 14.8cm x 21cm (A5), score it and fold it in half. Make an orange card blank the same size and score and fold it too.

2   With pencil, draw a chick in an egg shell over the fold of the cream card. Make sure the beak is evenly positioned. Draw over the lines with black fine liner pen to emphasise them.

3   Colour in the illustration with wax crayons. Mark a pattern on the egg. Use yellow to outline it, then with a pink crayon mark on wiggly lines. Using a red crayon, mark on spots. Colour in the beak and feet with an orange crayon. Mark on grass with different shades of green crayons. Colour the chick in yellow.

7   When the ink has dried, cut a slit with a craft knife across the centre of the beak.

8   Score the diagonal lines of the beak and push them forwards.

9   Cut around the frame and glue to the orange card. The beak will now look orange inside when it moves.

Wax Resist Origami Envelopes

To make a matching envelope, use the same wax resist technique that you used on the egg. Cover an A4 sheet in wax crayon patterns and then paint over them with ink. Leave this to dry and then fold the paper to make it into an origami envelope (see Envelopes section, pages 16–17). You could seal the flap with a melted wax crayon and deboss it with a child's printing tool.

4 Mark on clouds with a white wax crayon, using a scribbling motion.

5 Using a fine paintbrush, paint a purple frame with ink around the edge of the card. Paint over the egg with purple ink too.

6 Paint over the rest of the egg with blue ink. Dilute the ink with water to paint in the sky.

Other Easter Cards

Break Out

Make a card with an unhatched chick still in its egg. Draw the beak breaking out of the egg shell across the fold in the card. Mark lines on the egg for cracks in the shell.

Talking Chicks Triptych

Try making a triptych (three-sided card) as follows:

1 Cut a piece of cream laid card with an extra side (14.8cm x 31.5cm). You will need to use an A3 sheet of card for this. Score it and fold it twice. Do the same with an orange sheet of card.

2 Draw the egg and beak over the first fold and the chick in the egg over the second fold. Make the beaks smaller to allow the card to fold inwards.

3 Decorate with wax and ink as before.

4 Cut out and glue the image onto the orange card.

Flying Bat Card

Halloween

This rather batty Halloween card features a spooky creature of the night. He will fly out from the card and scare everyone in sight. This has been inspired by creepy stories where there always seems to be a daft bat or two in the belfry.

Children will love this card (especially those who are little horrors). His wiggly eyes will move as he flies around and make him appear comical. Children can help to make this card too. They could either make the bat or decorate the card with stars.

This card uses another type of v-fold cut. An arrow is glued on top of the v-fold and the bat is then glued to the arrow. The bat appears to fly as the card is opened and closed and the arrow moves up and down.

A Halloween colour scheme of purple, black, yellow and lime green is used. Stars are painted onto the purple card to make you think of a twilight scene.

There are templates for the bat body and wings at the back of the book as well as a template for the flying mechanism.

You Will Need

A4 black, lime, purple and yellow card

Craft knife

Ruler

Black felt tip pen

White and black acrylic paint

Paintbrush

Pencil

Scissors

Glue or glue stick

Wiggly eyes

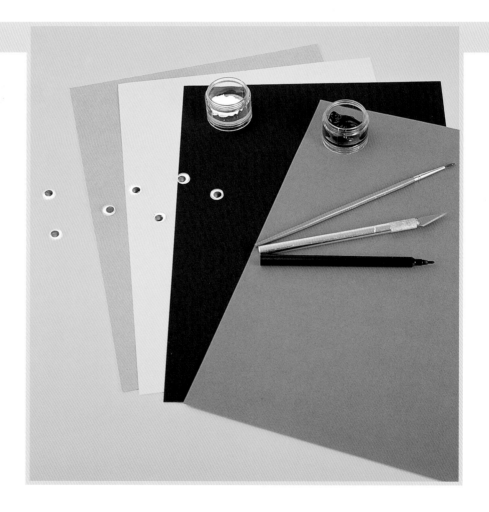

1   Score and fold the purple A4 sheet of card in half and draw stars on with a black felt-tip pen.

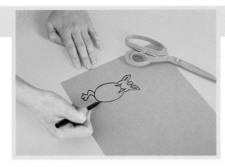

2   Draw the bat onto lime green card with a black felt-tip pen (use the template at the back of the book as a guide).

3   Cut out the bat and paint his body with black acrylic.

7   Colour in the stars with white paint.

8   When dry, fold the sheet of purple card in half and draw a diamond shape 5cm in length by 2cm in width. Position this 2cm from the top of the card. Draw the diamond on both sides of the card.

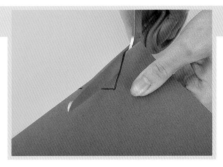

9   Cut the top line of the diamond while the card is folded

13   Glue the bat to the top of the arrow with a glue stick.

14   Finally, make a moon for the background by cutting a circle of yellow paper or card and gluing it to the top left-hand corner of the card.

4   Copy the template of the bat's wings onto black card, using a pencil and cut it out.

5   Paint lines onto the bat's wings with white paint and colour his fangs in white too.

6   Glue the bat's body to his wings and glue on two wiggly eyes.

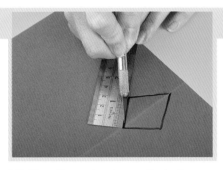

10   Open the card and score the bottom lines of the diamond with a ruler and a knife.

11   Cut an arrow (see template at the back of book) from purple card. The point of the arrow will be the same size as the diamond in step 8.

12   Push the diamond inwards to the front of the card and glue the arrow to the right-hand side of the diamond.

Other Flying Cards

A flying aeroplane card is perfect for a young boy's birthday. A flying stork carrying a bundle could celebrate a birth. Birds, insects, UFOs or even kites could be used to illustrate the card to suit the interests of the person who is going to receive it.

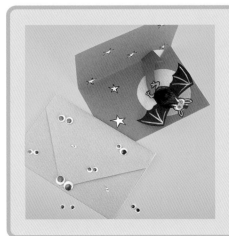

Spooky Envelope

You could make an origami envelope from an A3 sheet of lime-green or black paper. Secure the flap with wiggly eyes. Add other eyes to decorate and scare the recipient. They will look like eyes blinking in the dark.

Concertina Cards
Girlie Gift Card

Girl's Birthday

This is a quick and easy project that is great for using up scraps of cloth and leftover decoupage scraps. I've used playing cards to make unusual earrings and hairgrips. Girls of all ages will adore receiving them and enjoy wearing the gifts! If they don't have pierced ears (or you aren't sure they do) make a hairgrip or a brooch. This would make a suitable birthday card or could be sent to someone as a little gift; perhaps as a "thank you" or as a "get well soon".

Spotty polka dots will appeal to fans of the fantastic 1950s. The funky earrings would look great with a rock 'n' roll skirt or come in handy for cheating at poker! Queen of Hearts or the Ace of Spades?

Other types of printed fabric could be used to cover the card, scraps of striped, gingham, houndstooth, tartan or any other cloth with a retro style. Faces could be cut from decoupage scraps, magazines, photographs or postcards. You could use origami paper or hand decorated paper for the jewellery too.

The cards and jewellery are surprisingly quick to make. The only thing that takes time is waiting for the glitter fabric paint to dry. It may be a good idea to practise piping glitter onto a scrap of paper first. It is a bit like icing a cake!

You Will Need

A4 orange card

Ruler

Craft knife

Glue stick

Spotty fabric

Scissors

Image of a face. You can colour copy my
    drawing, or use decoupage scraps or
    a photo

Glittery fabric paint

Playing cards

Pin

Metal jewellery posts

Jewellery pliers

Earring wires

Metal hairgrip (optional)

Thin red ribbon

Tape or sticky labels

1   Make an orange A5 (14.8 by 21cm) card blank. Spread glue onto the front and back of the folded card. Lay the card on the reverse side of the fabric. Press it down firmly, ironing out any wrinkles with your hands.

2   Cut around the edge of the card with fabric scissors.

3   Cut out the image of the face you wish to use. Apply glue to the back of the image with a glue stick and position the image on the cloth covered card.

7   Slot a jewellery post through the hole.

8   Using pliers twist the wire around itself to secure the card in place.

9   Open out the loop at the bottom of the earring wire with pliers. Slot the hook onto the jewellery post and close it with the pliers.

Other Girlie Gift Cards

Hairgrip Gift Card

Cover a card in fabric, glue a face to it and pipe with glitter as before. Decorate a hair-grip by making a bow from a playing card. Concertina the card, this time tying it in the middle with a strip of cloth or ribbon. Glue it to the metal hairgrip with strong glue. Cut a slot in the fabric covered card so that the hairgrip will sit on the hair. Slide the hairgrip through the slot onto the card and onto the head.

4 Pipe the edge of the image with glitter glue. This will help secure the image to the cloth. Leave it to dry for as long as is suggested on the glitter paint bottle.

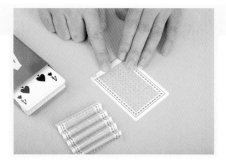

5 To make the earrings, fold a playing card into a concertina fan. Fold it one way and then the other at approximately 1cm intervals.

6 Pinch the fan together at one end and pierce it with a pin to make a hole right the way through the folds.

10 Decorate the earrings with bows made from thin red ribbon.

11 Finish the card with the handmade earrings by piercing through the card with a pin and pushing the earring wires through it. Add tape or sticky labels to the back to secure the earrings in place.

Pop-up Pouch Envelope

Make a pop-up pouch and stuff it with shredded paper to protect the gifts. Use corrugated card to correlate with the concertina effect of the gifts. This is also sturdy and protective for posting. Glue a playing card to the front of the pouch and use it as an address label. As a playing card is glossy, use a CD marker pen to write on it.

Bow Tie Brooch Card

You could also make a bow tie brooch in the same way. Glue a brooch back to the reverse of a concertina folded card that has been tied in the middle with a ribbon. To attach the brooch, make holes in the card and slot the pin of the brooch through them. Position it just under the chin like a real bow tie.

Fab Fairy Card

Party Invitations

Fairy, fairy, quite contrary! How do I make this card? With wrapping paper, lots of folding and a dash of sparkle – that's how.

This project is very simple to make but is bright and appealing. Use this card as an invitation for a party or as a birthday card. It has been made by using iridescent mirror card. The concertina folded skirt is reflected when the card is opened, making it look as though the skirt is a full circle. The fun element of the card will appeal to young girls, teenagers and the young at heart.

This card is inexpensive to make but the concertina effect of the coloured paper is strikingly effective when the card is opened. The fact that it is inexpensive will also make it suitable for party invitations just in case you have to make 50. The folding takes a little time to get right initially, but once you have mastered one, it is quick to produce more. If you have time, you could also make matching magic wands to give to party guests. An idea for making an envelope is included here, but if you are short of time try buying manufactured ones of the same size.

If you're not keen on fairies, how about ballerinas or colourful clowns? Sparkling jewels or fluffy feathers could also be added to the card. For the novice artists among us, it might be worth practising drawing a fairy on a scrap of paper before trying it on the actual card.

You Will Need

A4 iridescent mirror card (or similar
  card with a reflective finish)
Craft knife
Ruler
Black marker pen
Pink paint
Paintbrush
Stripy wrapping paper
Glue stick
Star stickers

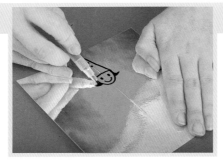

1 Make a card blank from a piece of iridescent mirror card 15cm x 15cm. Score and fold it in half.

2 Draw on the fairy with a black marker pen over the fold in the card. Draw a smiling face and pointy hat. Draw a chubby tummy, wings, legs and magic wand.

3 Then paint in the cheeks and tummy with pink acrylic paint and a paint brush.

7 Glue the concertinas to the card. Glue one side first and then stretch it across and glue the other. Glue the small concertina to the pointy hat and the larger one above the legs to create a skirt.

8 Decorate the card with star stickers. Add stickers to the hat, wand and tummy too.

Magic Fairy Wands

If you are throwing a children's party, you could make fairy wands to match the invitations and give them to the guest on their arrival. You could make two concertinas (skirts) and glue them together to create a fairy wand. You will need to stretch them out and glue them in the centre. Glue a star over the join to cover it and glue a stick behind the joined concertina so the wand can be waved. It is not really magic, but one can pretend!

  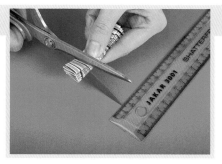

4 Take the wrapping paper and cut a strip 14cm x 24cm. Fold it in half and glue the two sides together to reinforce it and so that the concertina will be coloured on both sides.

5 Fold the strip at 1.5cm intervals, folding it one way and then the other until you reach the end.

6 Cut 1.5cm off the end of the folded concertina. This is for the brim of the hat.

Stripy Envelope

You could make a matching envelope from wrapping paper. Try making a straight, flapped envelope (16cm x 8cm) and line it with lilac paper. It could be lined with stripes on the inside or on the outside. Use matching star and heart stickers to seal the flap.

Making Striped Paper

If you can't find stripy wrapping paper or if you just want to make your card unique, make your own striped paper. Use plain white paper, together with felt tips and pencil crayons. Draw thin lines with different coloured felt-tips and colour in between them with pencil crayons. It will take some time to colour the stripes, but once you have made one sheet you could colour copy it. Don't forget that both sides need to be striped.

Valentine Hearts Card

Valentine's Day

This Valentine's card is made from cut-out chubby hearts. The concertina-style card gives depth to the cut outs and helps to create a tunnel effect. The hearts, which get smaller as you look into the tunnel, are sprayed with red and fluorescent pink paints. This card could be described as a "tunnel of love".

Brightly coloured spray paint and white card can look stunningly effective. Just don't get carried away and start spray-painting the walls. You could use blow pens or flick paint from an old toothbrush to achieve a similar effect. You could alter the colour scheme and try different variations of shapes if you want to send this card for an occasion other than Valentine's Day. Stars, flowers, trees, and simple snowflake shapes would look stunning cut from the concertina card.

This project requires a lot of accurate cutting with a craft knife and may require some practise first. The position of the hearts is also important in order to create a tunnel effect.

A template of concentric hearts is included at the back of the book. Trace them all onto tracing paper at the same time.

You Will Need

White card (A4 sheets x 2 or an A3
   sheet)
Glue
Craft knife
Cutting mat
Ruler
Pencil
Tracing paper x 2 sheets (one to trace
   the template on and the other to use
   for the envelope)
Craft spray paints: red, fluorescent pink

1   Cut a piece of white card 57cm x 21cm from an A3 sheet (or glue two pieces of A4 card together). Mark on 9.5cm panels, all the way along the card to make six panels in total.

2   Score along the panels and fold as you go. Fold one panel going one way and the next going the other way to create a concertina.

3   Fold all the sections of the card together. Trace the heart template at the back of the book. Trace the first heart onto the folded card. Make the bow of the heart 6cm from the top of the card.

7   Trace the third heart on to the third panel. Position it so that it will sit inside the two previous hearts and cut it out.

8   Repeat until you have cut out 5 concentric hearts. The final panel should be left blank. Open the card out. Lay it flat on the piece of paper you wish to use for the envelope (tracing paper has been used here).

9   Spray pink paint on the first and largest heart. Use a single spray close to the card. Try practising this on a scrap of paper first. The pink paint will be stencilled through the heart and onto the paper underneath.

4 Open the card out flat and lay it on a cutting mat. Cut the heart out with a craft knife.

5 Trace the second heart onto the second panel so that it will be positioned inside the first heart when the card is folded together.

6 Cut this heart out on a cutting mat.

10 Spray the second heart with red paint and the third with pink and so on.

11 Flip the card over and repeat the spraying in the same order on the other side. When you have reached the end panel, spray it red so that the smallest heart will have red behind it.

Valentine Hearts Envelope

Use the paper you laid under the card to make a matching envelope. The envelope will look fantastic. Not only has it been stencilled with the hearts, but the opaque nature of the tracing paper allows you to see through the envelope and show off the card. Use the straight-edged template to make an envelope to fit the card. Make it 11cm x 22cm.

Alternatively buy a DL envelope or banker envelope (see Glossary at the back of the book). Decorate it by laying the hearts you cut out of the card onto it and spraying paint over the top of them. To secure the envelope, use some clear tape.

Springy Garden Card

Birthday

Everyone feels special when they are given flowers. What better way to celebrate an occasion such as a birthday than with daisies. These crazy daisies are on stems constructed from concertinas, which allows them to spring out and surprise the recipient like a Jack-in-the-box. This is a great card for children or female relatives. Use it as a spring-time card or get well card. The jolly Jack-in-the-box flowers would really cheer someone up; he or she couldn't help but be charmed.

Plain lime green and yellow card has been drawn on with thick black outlines to create a comic book effect. The centres of the flowers have been made from circles cut from purple and cerise card.

This card is simple to make for adults and children alike. Children will enjoy making the concertina springs, which can be used in other craft projects too. All manner of Jack-in-the-boxes could be made by using the springs and gift boxes with lift off lids. How about a magician's rabbit-in-the-hat?

The template for the base of the card and its flaps can be found at the back of this book.

You Will Need

A4 lime green card and paper

Pencil

Ruler

Craft knife

Scissors

Glue stick

Yellow, purple and cerise card

Black felt-tip pen

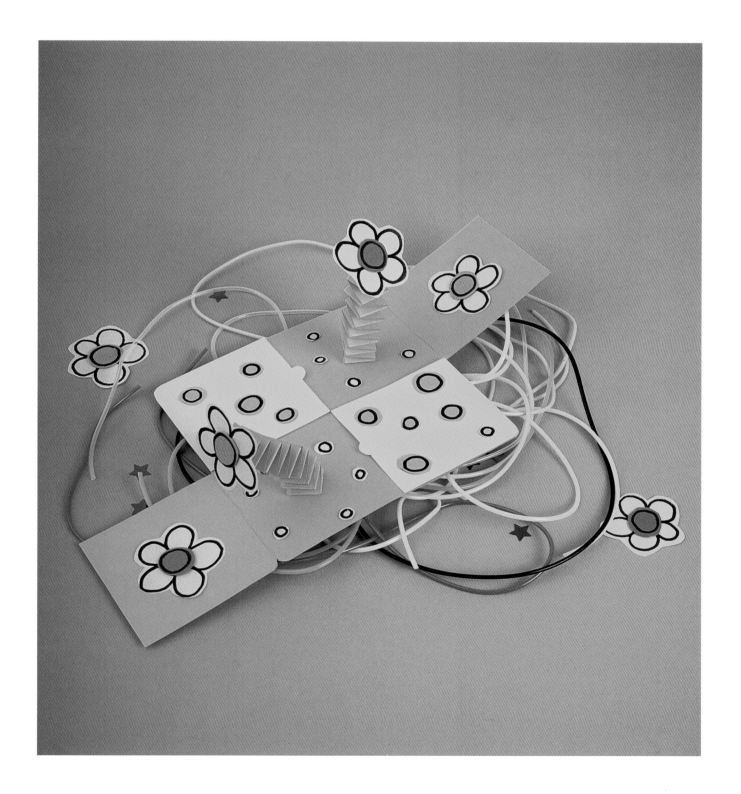

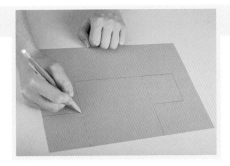

1 Start by copying the template of the base onto lime green card.

2 Copy the flap parts onto yellow card.

3 Cut out the yellow flaps and glue them onto the lime green base. Don't apply glue to the small curved sections. These need to be free to act as catches to allow the card to be folded up.

7 Cut out the small circles. Cut the 6 daisies and the 6 dots out. Glue the pink and purple circles to the centres of the flowers with a glue stick.

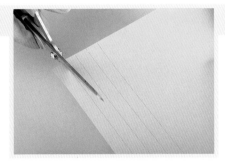

8 Cut four strips of lime green paper 1.5cm wide by the length of the longest side of the A4 paper.

9 Glue two of the strips together at right angles.

13 Glue dots to the card base: green dots on yellow card and yellow dots on green card.

Other Springy Cards

Try experimenting with bases made from different coloured card. You could make butterflies, ladybirds, bees, dragonflies or hummingbirds to accompany the flowers. Here a colour scheme of purple and pink has been used, but you could try thinking of other variations.

4 Cut out the base. Score and fold the sides inwards.

5 Using a black felt-tip pen draw six daisies and small circles onto leftover yellow card. Draw circles onto leftover lime card.

6 Then draw larger circles on cerise and purple card. Draw three on each colour.

10 Fold the left strip over the right strip and the right strip over the left strip. Keep folding one side over the other until you have formed a spring. Keep folding until you reach the end of each strip. Cut off any leftover paper.

11 Make another spring in the same way. Glue the ends of the springs to the centres of the green squares on the base of the card.

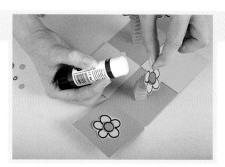

12 Glue flowers to the tops of the concertinas and to the fronts and insides of the flaps.

Spotty, Dotty Envelope

The flaps on the card allow you to squash the concertina flowers down. When the flaps are lifted, the flowers spring up. Write your message on the reverse side of the flat base of the card. Make a matching spotty, dotty envelope by gluing on hand drawn dots. I've used the template for the V-flap envelope (13.2 x 13.2cm) at the back of the book. Yellow and lime green card were glued back to back to make a two-tone envelope. Seal the flap with another cartoon flower, if you like.

Interactive Cards
Happy House Card

New Home

Make a happy house and put photos of your best friends inside it. Create shutters and doors that open out to reveal the photos hidden underneath. This jolly "advent calendar" style card can be sent to someone who is moving house. You could make the card to match their new home (even if they live in a flat) by making it in a different size or shape. This would make an unusual yet welcoming new home card.

The card could also be sent to friends or family who have moved away from your neighbourhood. It could be used simply as a "Hello" or "Don't forget me" card. Stick photos of yourself and your family behind the shutters and send to a relative in a far away place to act as a reminder of the folks back home.

This attractive project is made from smooth, colourful card decorated with a collage of paper and acrylic paints. The colour scheme of bright yellow, orange and lime is cheerful and will put the recipient in a good mood.

For different variations, make a church with a bride and groom inside as a wedding card. For a Christmas card make a snow covered cottage that has shutters, which open to reveal a festive scene inside. People could be silhouetted against the warm glow of a log fire.

Children will be able to decorate this card, but an adult will need to be on hand to do the cutting with a craft knife. The door and shutters are cut on three sides. The fourth side is uncut and acts as a hinge.

You Will Need

A4 yellow card

Craft knife

Ruler

Orange, lime green, purple and cerise
    paper

Scissors

Glue stick

Pencil

Acrylic paints: green, blue and crimson

Paintbrush

Tape

Photos of friends and family

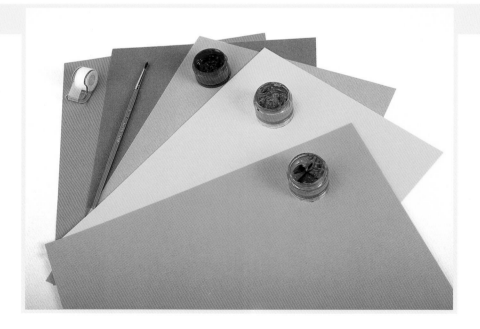

1 Take an A4 sheet of yellow card, score it and fold it in half.

2 Cut two triangles from the corners of the card to make a roof shape.

3 Lay the card on top of orange paper and draw around it to make an orange roof.

7 Mark lines on the roof, shutters, door and tulips with a pencil.

8 Paint over the pencil lines with crimson paint. Paint in tulips and the shutters in the roof as well.

9 Paint the shutters and door blue.

13 Tape pieces of card to the backs of the windows to make curtains. Tape pictures of friends behind the shutters.

Happy House Envelope

Make an orange straight-edged envelope C5 size (16.2cm x 22.9cm) and paint it to match the stripes on the roof. Paint wiggly lines where the address will go. You could also paint a tulip on the envelope to match the card.

4 Cut out the roof shape and scallop the edge by waving the scissors as you are cutting it.

5 Glue the roof to the card with a glue stick.

6 Cut a strip of lime green grass and glue it on to the base of the card.

10 Colour in the leaves of the tulips with green paint.

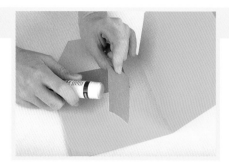

11 Leave the paint to dry, then glue pieces of cerise and purple paper onto the reverse of the card where the shutters and door are to line them.

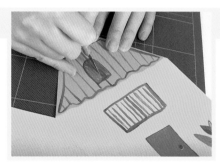

12 Turn over and lay the card flat on a cutting mat. Score cuts in the door and shutters, leaving one edge uncut to make a hinge.

Other House Cards

Use brick-patterned paper, which can be bought from a doll-house specialist. Use photos of friends or draw caricatures of them to glue behind the shutters. Some may be glued to the back of the card to add an extra dimension. How about making a doghouse to hold pictures of your furry friends?

Spinning Shoes Card

Thanks

All shoe-loving women will adore this card, as the colour of the cut out shoe changes every time you spin the wheel. The finished card has a decadent look, with its use of shimmering gold card and colourful gift-wrap. In fact it is a great way to use up leftover scraps of wrapping paper and trimmings.

This card could be used to say thank you or made as an invite to your friends for a girls' night out or a day of shopping. I have customised the card using thin pink ribbon, but it can be styled to suit the recipient's taste, by using glitter, sequins or stick on jewels. Different coloured papers could also be used. Do you know someone who is mad about red shoes or crazy about leopard prints? What shoes to wear? It is such a tough decision for a girl!

This project is easy to make and there is a template of the shoe at the back of the book.

You will need

A4 gold card

Craft knife

Ruler

Pencil

Scissors

Glue Stick

4 types of patterned wrapping paper

Sticky fixer pads

Scraps of card

Brass fastener or split pin

Thin pink ribbon

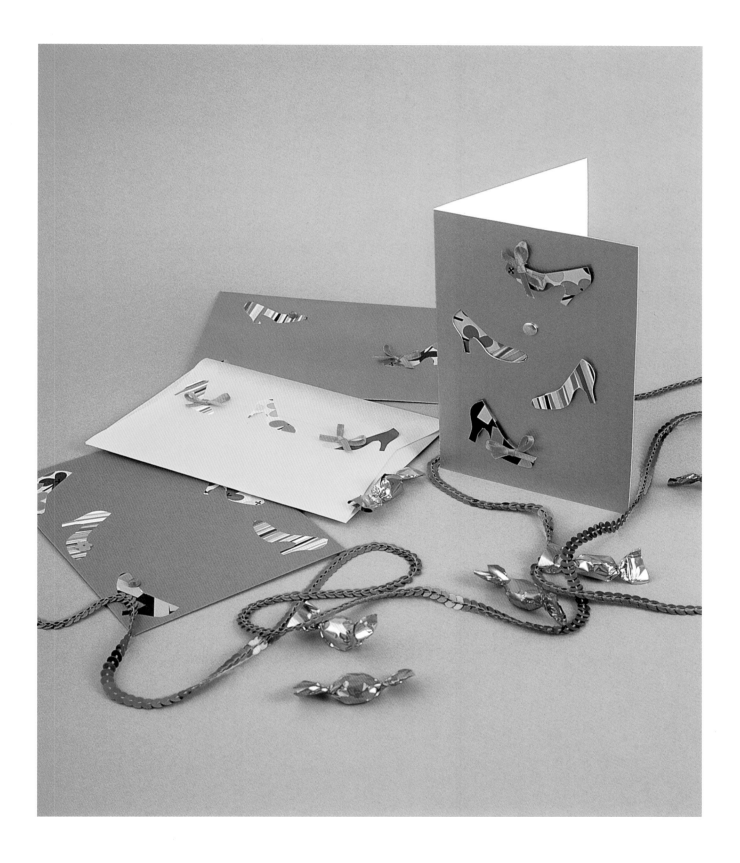

1   Make a card blank 14.8cm x 21cm (A5) from the gold card and score and fold it in half.

2   Draw a shoe on a scrap of card to make a template. Make the shoe roughly 4.5cm x 2.5cm and cut it out with scissors.

3   Glue three pieces of different wrapping paper onto scraps of card to strengthen them.

7   Attach the three cut-out shoes to the front of the card with sticky fixer pads. The sticky pads will need to be cut down to size first.

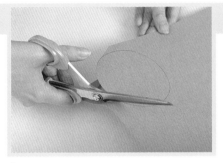

8   Draw a circle 9.5cm in diameter on a scrap of card and cut it out.

9   Divide the circle into four using a ruler and pencil. Then glue on four different styles of wrapping paper with a glue stick. Cut off any excess wrapping paper.

Shoe Envelopes

Make a straight-edged envelope C6 (11.4cm x 16.2cm) and decorate it with shoes cut from different styles of wrapping paper. Decorate with bows, sequins or gem stones. You could decorate the front of the envelope and use cut out shoes to seal the back.

If you are giving the card to someone for their birthday, wrap their present in the same wrapping paper to co-ordinate the gift and card.

4 Draw around the shoe stencil onto the back of the card covered in wrapping paper. Cut out three shoes in different patterns.

5 Draw the shoe on the front of the card. The heel should be approx. 7.5cm from the base.

6 Open the card out flat and lay it on a cutting mat. Cut out the shoe with a craft knife. You may need to practise this first.

10 Place the wheel behind the cut out shoe on the card. Position it so that the shoe is covered at all times. Push a split pin or brass fastener through the card and through the wheel. Open the arms of the pin to secure the wheel.

11 Tie some tiny bows from the thin pink ribbon. Finish the card by gluing them onto a couple of the shoes.

Other Spinning Wheel Cards

How about trying a spinning wheel card featuring different items of clothing, such as mini skirts, hot pants, T-shirts, dresses, undies or handbags. You could make a masculine version featuring ties or socks. What about trying a different style of shoe, like a Mary Jane, a ballet pump, a flip-flop or even a Wellington boot.

Wiggling Hula Girl Card

Bon Voyage

Know a friend who is going on a trip to a tropical island? Hawaii, perhaps? You could use this card as a bon voyage card, since the Hula girl will put anyone in the right mood for an exotic holiday. The dancing girl wiggles when you pull the tabs and her grass skirt wafts in the breeze. Fabric flowers are used to make a necklace, or Lei as it is called in Hawaii. A flower has also found its way into her hair. Hula girl is a tireless dancer and will sway her hips to whatever music is on the radio. She likes the ukulele best, but I've seen her move to hardcore techno.

This project is slightly more complicated to make, compared with others in this book. The card blank needs to have slots cut into it and a pull tab mechanism needs to be made. The legs of the hula girl slot through from the front to the inside of the card. They then slot through a cut in the pull-tab. To help you, there are templates located at the back of the book for the girl and the pull-tab.

You Will Need

A4 yellow card x 2	Scissors
Craft knife	Acrylic paints: pink, cream, brown,
Ruler	orangey red
Glue stick	Paint brush
Tracing paper	Lime green paper
Pencil	Wavy edged scissors
White card	Fabric flowers
Black felt-tip pen	Sticky double-sided pads

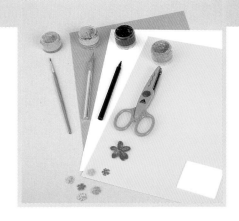

1   Start by scoring and folding an A4 piece of yellow card in half.

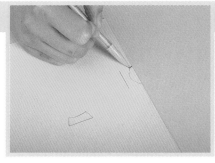

2   Mark the position of the slots, as shown in the template at the back of the book.

3   Lay the card flat on a cutting mat and cut out the slots.

4   Copy the "pull-tab" template at the back of the book onto yellow card.

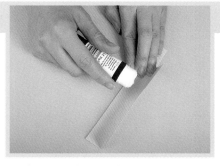

5   Score the fold line, fold the top part over and glue it with a glue stick to re-inforce it.

6   Use the knife to cut a slot in the centre of the strip, through both pieces of card.

7 Fold the lines at the end of the strip inward, so that the end looks curved.

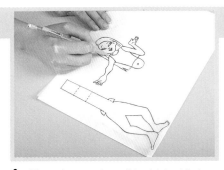

8 Trace the template of the Hula girl's legs and body onto white card.

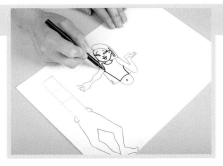

9 Draw over the lines with a black felt-tip pen to emphasise them.

13 Open out the card. Slot the pull-tab through the slit in the side of the card blank. Apply glue to the tab at the curled end of the pull tab. Check the positioning is right and press down the pull tab to the inside of the card by curling under and gluing it, just before the crease in the card.

14 Fold the tabs on the legs to the back of the card. Thread the legs through the slot in the front of the card and open out the tabs on the back. Thread the flap through the slot in the pull-tab strip. Thread the flap back through the front of card so that the legs are secured.

15 Make a hula skirt from a piece of lime green paper. Cut the hem with wiggly scissors.

Wiggle Motion

The bottom half of the girl will now move or wiggle from side to side when the tab is pulled! She won't go crazy and do cartwheels, but she will wiggle playfully to and fro.

Other Wiggling Cards

Make a card in another colour or cut the edges with wiggly scissors. Once you have mastered making the mechanism, try other variations. Try a ballerina, a footballer or a maybe a wiggling Elvis impersonator.

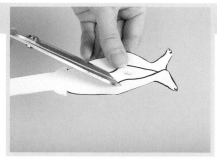

10 Cut out the legs, including the space between them.

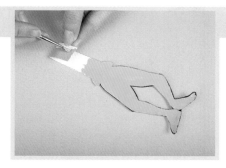

11 Paint them with cream paint. Fold over the top flap. Paint the folded over part of the flap with cream paint too.

12 Paint the upper body with cream, brown and orangey red paint. Leave to dry.

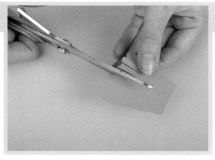

16 Snip upwards with straight scissors to create the look of a grass skirt. Bend and crinkle the grass strips so that they look uneven and more grass-like.

17 Decorate the girl with a necklace of flowers. Glue a flower in her hair too.

18 Glue the grass skirt over the legs with a glue stick. Attach the girl's body to the card with sticky fixer pads.

Floral Envelope

Make a straight-flapped envelope to the dimensions of C5 (16.2 x 22.9cm). Decorate it by gluing colourful fabric flowers in each of its corners to echo the floral Lei worn by the Hula girl. Use glued flowers to seal the flap too.

Cry Baby Card

New Baby

This cartoon character baby is part of an interactive set of cards. If it is crying it can be shushed by slotting the dummy into its mouth. The card could be given to celebrate a new birth, or the same principle could be applied to other themes – someone eating chocolate, ice cream or a slice of birthday cake perhaps? It also could be adapted for an animal lover. What about a penguin with a fish in its mouth, a rabbit munching on a carrot, or a panda chewing on a stick of bamboo?

The baby's face appears to pop out of the card, which is achieved by a simple box and hinge mechanism. The baby's face is almost entirely cut away from the card, leaving only the section in the hinge uncut. This card is easy to make, but requires some precise cutting with a craft knife. There is a template of the baby's face and dummy at the back of the book. Also presented is an idea for making an envelope, but if you are short of time buy manufactured ones to the same size and decorate it in the same way to match.

You will need

A3 cream coloured card

Pencil

Ruler

Scissors

Medium-sized paint brush

Acrylic paints: cream, lime green, white, pink

Black felt-tip pen

Craft knife

0.5m of yellow ribbon

Glue stick

Daisy sequins without holes

1 Cut a piece of cream card, 15cm x 30cm, to make a square card blank. Don't fold it. Leave it flat and mark on the centre with a few dashes.

2 Draw the baby's face in the centre of the card with a pencil about. 2.5cm from the top of the card (see template at the back of the book). Draw on the hinge part too, using a fainter line.

3 On a leftover scrap of flesh coloured card, draw a dummy and a curl of hair.

7 Go over the lines with a black felt-tip pen to accentuate them. Using a craft knife, cut around the face – leaving the box uncut to act as a hinge. Cut out the right ear, up to the vertical line.

8 Cut a slit in the top of the mouth to accommodate the dummy.

9 Cut the dummy out (including the space in the handle). Cut out the curl of hair.

13 Thread the dummy and ribbon from the back of the card through to the front. Pull the raw edge of the ribbon out behind the baby's cut out ear. Glue the ribbon under the green border on the card. Cut off any leftover ribbon and then glue it on to the other side of the card.

4 Mark a point 6cm down from the top of card. Draw a horizontal line (omitting the baby's face) across the card from this point. Then paint the background above the line with green paint and a medium sized brush.

5 Paint the face with cream coloured paint. Add white to the eyes and pink to the cheeks.

6 Colour in the curl of hair with black felt-tip pen. Paint the dummy with the acrylic paints. Add white highlights and pink to add depth.

10 Make a bow from yellow ribbon. Glue the curl of hair to the underside of the baby's head and glue the bow over the top.

11 Thread the end of the ribbon through the handle on the dummy and glue it to its underside.

12 Glue daisy sequins to the green background using a glue stick.

Boy or Girl Card

The colour scheme can be altered to be gender specific with either pastel blues or pinks. If you want to make the card suitable for both genders (if you are making it in advance of the birth), try lime green or a lemon yellow. Use pastel coloured ribbons and hand tied bows to complement the colour scheme.

Square Cry Baby Envelope

Make a square envelope using the v-flap template. Make it 15.6 x 15.6cm. Paint a dummy in one of the corners and add a border around the edge.

Pop-up Cards
Pop-up Plant Pot

Just to Say

Sometimes you need a cheerful card just to say, "hello" or "how are you?" These cards are just the job. Make them in advance and keep them just in case you need a colourful little card.

The pop-up element is simple to create. The decoration will take a bit longer. It can be adapted to suit personal tastes or to match a friend's favourite type of flowers.

Two card blanks have been glued, one inside the other, to create a two-tone effect card. The backing card will show through the opened out vase. Glue the cards together along the creases and keep the pages loose to create a booklet effect. For an extra touch, you could spray a floral perfume in between the two layers of card.

Try making cards of different colours or differently shaped flower punches. Alter the colours and patterns on the pot, or alter the shape of the pot to turn it into a vase. Have three flowers sticking out, or go crazy and have thirty.

The pop-up principle could be applied to all manner of cards. How about a person reading a book? The book should be made in the same way as the vase. Draw a person behind the pop-out section. Draw hands on the book holding it up to their face. Perhaps they are reading a book on pop-up cards.

You Will Need

Cerise and purple A4 card

Craft knife

Ruler

Pencil

Scissors

Lime green, pink and silver acrylic paint

Daisy and butterfly craft punch

Cerise, red, lilac and orange papers

Single-hole punch

1   Make an A5 (14.8 x 21cm) card blank from purple card and another the same size from cerise card.

2   Take the folded purple card and measure 6.5cm down the spine. Draw a line 3cm across from this point.

3   Measure 4.25cm down from this point and draw a line 1.5cm across.

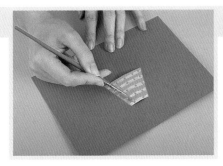

7   Paint on silver lines and pink dots.

8   Take the craft punch and cut 3 red, 4 cerise, 2 orange and 1 lilac daisy. Take the hole punch and cut 10 dots in a mixture of colours.

9   Glue the dots to the centre of the daisies.

13   Glue the spine of the finished purple card inside the crease of the cerise card. The cerise card will show through the gap in the plant pot.

Other Pop-up Plant Pot Colour Schemes

Pink and Orange

For an alternative colour scheme, make the card in the same way, but use pink card inside orange card. Punch out purple and lilac flowers and use orange and pink dots for the centres.

Orange and Purple

Make the card in the same way, but this time decorate it with flowers cut from a differently shaped hole punch. Use dots of pink paint for their centres.

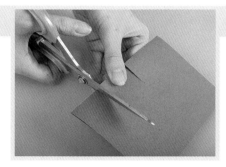

4 Cut along both of the horizontal lines with scissors.

5 Draw a diagonal line between the two cuts and score with a ruler and a knife. Turn the card over and score the same line on the reverse side.

6 Open the card, push the pot forward and paint it with lime green acrylic.

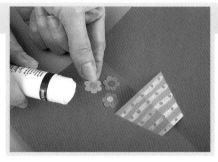

10 Glue the daisies to the card above the plant pot.

11 Add dots of pink paint to the centres of the flowers.

12 Finish the card with a butterfly cut from orange paper.

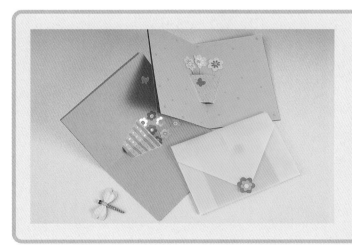

Origami Flower Envelopes

Make an origami envelope (see Envelope section, pages 16–17) with opaque paper and put any leftover punched shapes into the envelope. They will show through the translucent paper. Use flowers, butterflies and dots to co-ordinate with the finished card. Close the flap by gluing punched out shapes over the point.

Cool Lettering Card

Teenage Birthday

This is a perfect card for teenage birthdays. Cool dudes and hipsters will appreciate it. It's like, umm, y'know, kinda cool man!

This card is very simple to make and is based upon a box cut. It is also inexpensive to create as you can use plain white card and leftover wallpaper, combined with lettering cut from holographic card to add a touch of colour and sparkle. Mirrored, glossy, fluorescent or metallic card could be used instead, anything that will look modern or futuristic.

Use wallpaper to line the inside of the card. Different textured papers could be used to make this card appear more 3-D and funky. A colour scheme of white and dark blue looks simple, clean and slick.

Fans of mobile phone text messaging would appreciate this card too. You will be limited by the amount of letters (due to the size of the card) you can use, so you could abbreviate words. Try cutting messages and slogans from card, such as U R GR8, LUV U or 4EVER.

You Will Need

A4 white card

White embossed wallpaper

Scissors

Ruler

Glue stick

Craft knife

Pencil

Blue holographic card

1   Cut a piece of white card, 12cm x 24cm. Cut wallpaper the same size and glue the two pieces together with a glue stick.

2   Fold it in half and mark four strips on the reverse (make them slightly different lengths) approximately 3–4cm in length and 1cm wide.

3   Cut the strips while the card is still folded. Cut through the spine of the card.

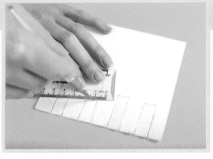

4   Score the horizontal lines on both sides of the card.

5   Open the card and push the strips forwards.

6   On the reverse of the holographic card, draw lettering and a star. Make sure it is mirror imaged so that it will be the right way around when cut.

7   Cut out and glue the lettering to the strips.

8   Finish the card with a star glued in the background.

Age Cards

It is always someone's birthday, so you could make age cards to celebrate specific mile stone birthdays such as 18 and 21. You could make age cards for friends and relatives of all ages. You will only need one or two strips, unless the recipient is going to be 100. Draw the numbers onto the reverse of the card you wish to use. Remember to mirror image the numbers so that, when they are cut, they are the correct way round.

Cool Envelopes

Make a lined envelope with blue paper and wallpaper using the v-flap template at the back of the book. Make it 13.2cm x 13.2cm. Close the flap with a cut out star.

Handbag

Female Relative

We all know someone who loves shopping. Shopaholics will appreciate this card, as will anyone who loves handbags. Give this card to your mum for Mother's Day or send it to a girl friend who is always swinging a different bag.

Strings of sequins are glued around the edge of the bag for dazzling effect. Flower sequins decorate one side of the card's edge and a matching flower sequin has been glued to the bag to look like a clasp.

You will need to use card that has been printed on both sides. Make handbags using different types of printed card, leopard print or cow hide. If you can't find animal card try painting animal print patterns onto plain card. Animal print stencils can be bought and used with spray paint or a stencil brush and paint. Failing that, you could use textured paper to make it look like leather or mock crock.

There is a template for the bag and handle at the back of the book. It is a very simple card to make. The only tricky bit is cutting the slits for the handles. The template could be altered, you could try creating bags of different shapes and sizes. You could also use a briefcase or a suitcase, if something more manly is required.

The tabs of the bag are glued around the crease of the card, which means the bag will become 3-D when the card is opened wide. The card blank acts as a base and is another version of a double page pop-up as with the Hollywood Cocktail project.

You Will Need

A4 pale pink card blank

Craft knife

Ruler

A4 black and white animal print card

Strong glue

Silver glitter glue

String of sequins in pale pink

Flower sequins

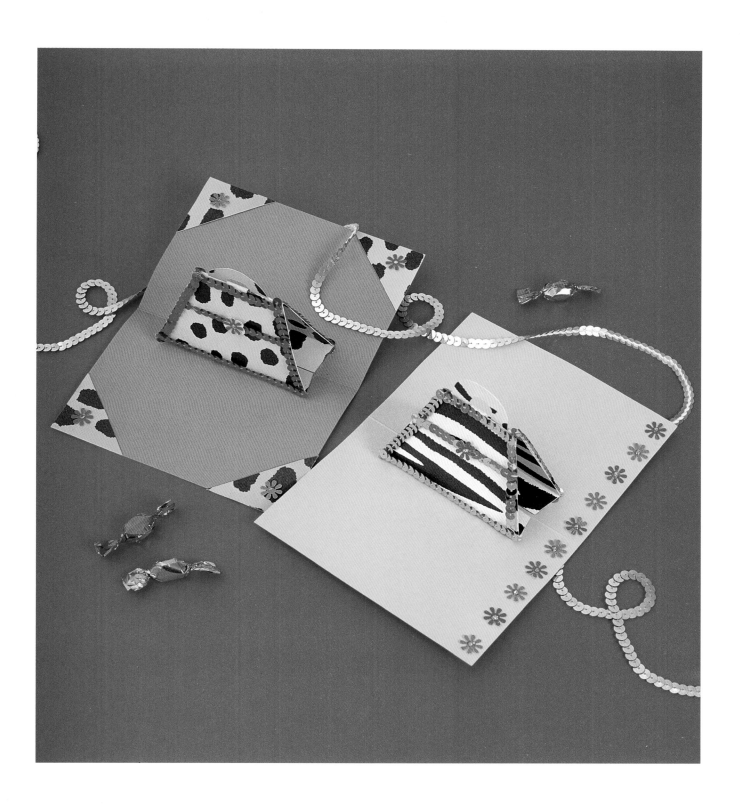

1   Start by making an A5 (14.8cm x 21cm) card blank from pale pink card.

2   Copy the template of the handbag onto animal print card. Copy the handle too.

3   Cut them both out with scissors.

7   Cut the slots with a knife. This is a fold-cut.

8   Push the handle through the slots. It needs to be tight so that it won't move about.

9   Using strong glue, stick the string of sequins around the edge of the bag. Glue them along the top and bottom. Finish by gluing across the front (approx. 2.5cm from the top edge).

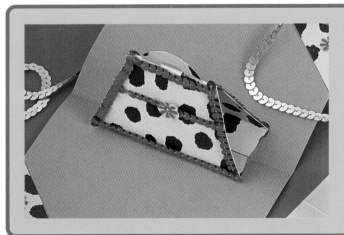

Leopard Print Handbag

This card has been made in the same way, but just uses a different colour scheme. The handbag has been made by using leopard print card and a cerise pink string of sequins. The dark pink card base has been decorated with leftover triangles of leopard print card glued into each of the corners.

4 Mark on score lines and graze the card with a knife.

5 Fold the tabs inwards.

6 Mark on the slots for the handles 1cm in from the edge of the bag. Each slot should be 1cm wide.

10 Decorate the card with a row of flower sequins, glued on with glitter glue.

11 Glue the tabs on the handbag to the flattened card. Centre them at the crease.

12 Glue a flower sequin to the front of the bag with glitter glue.

Animal Print Envelope

For the envelope, you could photocopy a sheet of card and use it to make an animal print envelope. You will need to use an A4 sheet to make a C6 (11.4cm x 16.2cm) envelope. Copy the straight-edged envelope template at the back of the book. Use an address label edged with sequins on the front. Decorate the flap on the back with a string of sequins too. Before posting it, remember to write your message on the underside of the card.

3-D Tree Card

Winter Holidays

Christmas just wouldn't be Christmas without a tree. These festive trees are perfect for the winter holidays. Use traditional red and green Christmas colours or make them from metallic or holographic card. I have decked the trees with dots cut from the edge of the card. Pencils and felt tips have also been used to decorate the tree. My tree has a smiling face, which would appeal to children, but this could be omitted if you are sending it to older relatives.

In addition, trees could be decorated with strings of sequins or tinsel pipe cleaners. Trees could also be made to look snowy by adding white paint and touches of glitter. You could add a gold star to the top by of the tree by drawing it onto the template.

These cards are easy to make. The trees are in two halves and slot together to make an "X" shape. When the card is opened, the tree opens and becomes 3-D. The tree then folds down to become totally flat. Some care needs to be taken when positioning and gluing the tabs of the tree into place. If they are not in the right spot, the card will fail to open and close correctly; get it right and you will want to make lots more.

The same principle could be applied to a star shape that could be used for a birthday or congratulatory card with wording, "Well done. You are a Star!" There is a template at the back of the book for the tree.

You Will Need

A4 red card

Craft knife

Ruler

Tracing paper

Pencil

A4 lime green card

Pencil crayons

Black felt tip

Single hole punch

Glue stick

1 Make a card blank 26cm by 11cm from red card and score and fold it in half.

2 Copy the template of the tree (see the back of the book) onto tracing paper. Make the tree 9cm in length. Copy the tree onto lime green card.

3 Turn the tracing paper over and draw a mirror image of the tree. Don't forget to mark on the tabs.

7 Open the tree out flat and colour in the branches with a green pencil crayon.

8 Open the other sides of the tree and colour them in green too.

9 Mark on a face and presents with a black felt-tip pen. Colour the presents in with pencils.

Other 3-D Tree Cards

You could leave the trees undecorated for a simple, understated look. This will be quicker too, if you are planning on making cards to send to everyone you know. Use holographic card and punch out holes from around the card to decorate the tree for a dazzling effect.

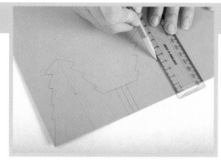

4 Mark slots on the central line of the tree 4.5cm in length.

5 Cut both trees out and also the slots. Cut one slot going up one tree and the other slot going down the other tree.

6 Slot the two trees together.

10 Cut holes around the edge of the card with a single hole punch.

11 Glue the cut out dots to the tree to make baubles.

12 Score the tabs and glue them to the tree (approximately 7cm apart) so that the tree will sit comfortably when opened and closed.

Tree Card Envelope or Pouch

Make a v-flap envelope (13.2 x 13.2cm). You could make it two-tone by lining red crepe paper (with holes punched out of it) with lime green paper on the underside. You could also make a red pop-up pouch from holographic card. Stuff it with shredded green paper.

Walking the Dog Card

Birthday

The inspiration behind this card lies in long autumnal walks in the park with a dog on a lead. This illustrated pooch is straining at the leash and appears to have left his muddy paw prints all over the place! This card is called Walking the Dog but just who is walking whom?

This is an ideal card for dog lovers. The colour scheme of red, black and lime green makes it suitable for men and women, young or old. You could send one to a friend who has walked your dog for you. You could even send one to your pet!

The colour scheme could be altered, as could the breed of the dog. How about a poodle stamped on pink card, a Scotty dog wearing a coat or a sausage dog on a long thin card blank? You could even make a fish on a line for a fishing fanatic.

The dog is glued to a simple box fold. It is an incredibly easy card to make, although the decoration takes time. Making the foam rubber stamp takes time initially, but makes it easy to duplicate the card again. If you don't have foam rubber, you could always cut the dog and paw from layers of felt. If you are feeling more energetic, a lino print could be carved and would last longer. Templates for the dog and paw are at the back of the book.

You Will Need

Craft knife

Ruler

A3 red card

Tracing paper

Pencil

Funky foam (any colour)

Scissors

Ballpoint pen

Glue stick

Old lids or jar tops: one big, one small

Black stamp pad

Wire

Black acrylic

Paintbrush

Lime green card

Red sequins for collar

1 Cut a piece of red card 16.5cm by 28cm, score it and fold it in half.

2 Trace the images of the dog and paw print onto tracing paper. Transfer the images onto pieces of foam by retracing the lines onto the foam.

3 Cut the dog out of the foam. Cut the head away from the body. Cut the paw out of foam also.

4 Using the ballpoint pen, make an oval dent in the foam for the dog's eye.

5 Glue the dog onto a large, flat lid, leaving a gap between the head and body.

6 Glue the paw onto a smaller lid (a round one if you can find one). Space the toes around the paw pad to divide them.

7 Measure along the spine of the card to halfway or 8.25cm and make a mark. Draw a box, 3cm x 5cm, so that it is centred on the mark.

8 Cut along the 3cm lines with scissors, through the spine of the card.

9 Score along the 5cm line on both sides of the card with a craft knife.

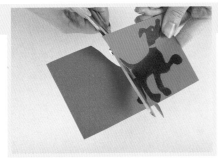

13 Stamp the dog onto a scrap of red card and cut it out.

14 Glue the dog shape to the front of the box.

15 Wiggle a piece of wire to make it into a wavy lead. Paint it with black acrylic.

Paw Print Envelope

To make a shop bought envelope seem original, stamp paws on the back of it too. You will need to use a C5 (16.2 x 22.9cm) envelope that can accommodate the card or make your own envelope to those dimensions. Stamp it to make it look walked over by a dog. Stamp around the edge or just stamp a single paw on the flap.

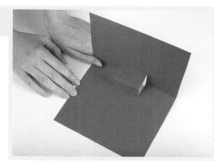

10 Open the card and push the box in.

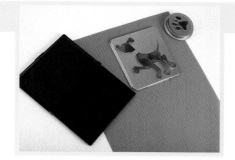

11 Apply ink to the dog and paw stamps and practise stamping them on a scrap of paper.

12 Re-ink the paw stamp and press it down along the edge of the card blank. Turn it one way and then the other to create a more varied effect.

16 Make a collar from a scrap of card and sequins. Glue the collar and the lead to the dog.

Handy hint

To clean the stamp, run it under water and wash it with washing-up liquid. Leave it to dry naturally without rubbing it, so as not to damage the surface of the stamp.

Walkies Stationery Set

How about making matching stationery? You could try different coloured papers or experimenting with different coloured inks. Decorate the notepaper and envelopes to co-ordinate them. You can make it look as though the paper has been walked across by stamping two feet side by side, one slightly higher than the other, then repeating it across the envelope.

Wedding Cake Card

Wedding

This card looks good enough to eat. The cake looks as though it has been intricately constructed, but really it is made from simple cuts and scores. The card is divided into sections that are cut to create steps. The steps cast shadows as light shines through the back of the card. The card is mainly white, but touches of silver, gold and handmade paper add interest and texture. It makes a perfect wedding card.

Handmade paper isn't always suitable for making pop-up cards, as it doesn't score or fold well, but it has been used here for decorative purposes. The paper enhances the look of the design and softens sharp edges.

You could adapt its three-tiered box effect to make a castle, waterfall or pile of Christmas presents. You could try a "moving house" card with heaped up piles of boxes marked with the word "Fragile".

You Will Need

A4 white card

Craft knife

Ruler

Pencil

Scissors

Handmade paper (petals or metallic)

Glue stick

Silver card

Star sequins

1   Make a card blank, 21cm x 16cm, score and fold. Cut the handmade paper to the same size.

2   While the card blank is folded, mark it half way along and draw a box, 6cm x 3.5cm. Draw another box on top of this, 4cm x 2.5 cm, and another box on top of this, 2cm x 1.5cm.

3   Keep the card blank folded and cut up to the first horizontal line.

4 Score the horizontal line and flip over and score it on the reverse.

5 Open the card and push the box forwards.

6 Fold the card with the box still pushed inwards. Cut the second box up to the horizontal line.

10 Use a pencil mark to make ribbon swags. Mark on icing and curls at the top of the cake too.

11 Cut varying sizes of hearts from the handmade paper.

12 Glue the hearts to the cake with a glue stick.

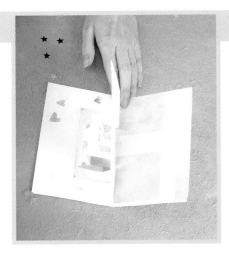

16 Finish by gluing the piece of handmade paper to the back of the card. This will show through the gap in the cake and cover pencil marks.

Other Cake Cards

You could make another cake by using a different type of handmade paper. For an alternate version of the cake, hearts have been cut from handmade paper, but only from the areas that had pressed petals trapped inside the pulp.

7 Score a horizontal line on both sides.

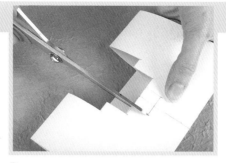

8 Push the box forwards to the inside of the card. Repeat cutting and scoring with the third box

9 Open the card and push the third box forwards.

13 Draw a cake base from silver card to fit around the bottom box. Make it 10.5cm x 8cm, with a centre, 6cm x 3.5cm. Cut out the cake base.

14 Glue to the card at the base of the cake and glue hearts to the bottom of the card.

15 Add a star sequin to the top of the cake.

Wedding Card Envelopes

Make a straight-edged envelope from matching handmade paper. If you have time, you could also line the envelope with silver, gold or pink paper. Gold or silver sealing wax could be used to seal the flap. Try to get hold of initial seals with the couple's initials and use them to press into the wax. You could always give them the seals as a wedding gift!

TV Card

Male Relative

Is that our Rover on the news? What has he done? Learned to bark Happy Birthday? Or perhaps he is going to be the canine star in a remake of *Lassie*?

This card will appeal to both male and female members of the family. All ages can appreciate this card. Make it for your dad if he is something of a TV addict, or notorious for keeping hold of the remote control. It would be a fun and thoughtful card for Father's Day. Use a comical canine picture, a picture of a celebrity, sporting team or family member. If you are struggling to find wood-effect card, DIY stores often stock wood-effect, sticky backed plastic which you can stick to a sheet of card. Failing that, you could glue a colour copy to a piece of card to stiffen it. Glossy black or metallic card could be used too.

If you don't know any TV addicts, perhaps you know a computer geek? You could adapt this idea to look like a computer monitor. Make a keyboard and a mouse out of a separate piece of card and glue them to the card blank. I'm sure you will know someone with square eyes.

This is a complicated project that requires you to score and fold card into the shape of a box. Copy the template on the last page of the book onto the reverse side of your wood-effect card. It can be scaled up or down to create boxes of different sizes, but the measurements need to be accurate for it to work well. It also needs to be positioned correctly on the card to allow easy folding. It is a good idea to make a practice card from scrap first.

You Will Need

A4 pale green card

Craft knife

Ruler

Pencil

A4 wood-effect card

Tracing paper

Scissors

Black marker pen

Image of pet, celebrity or family
  member

Double sided tape

Silver card

Glue stick

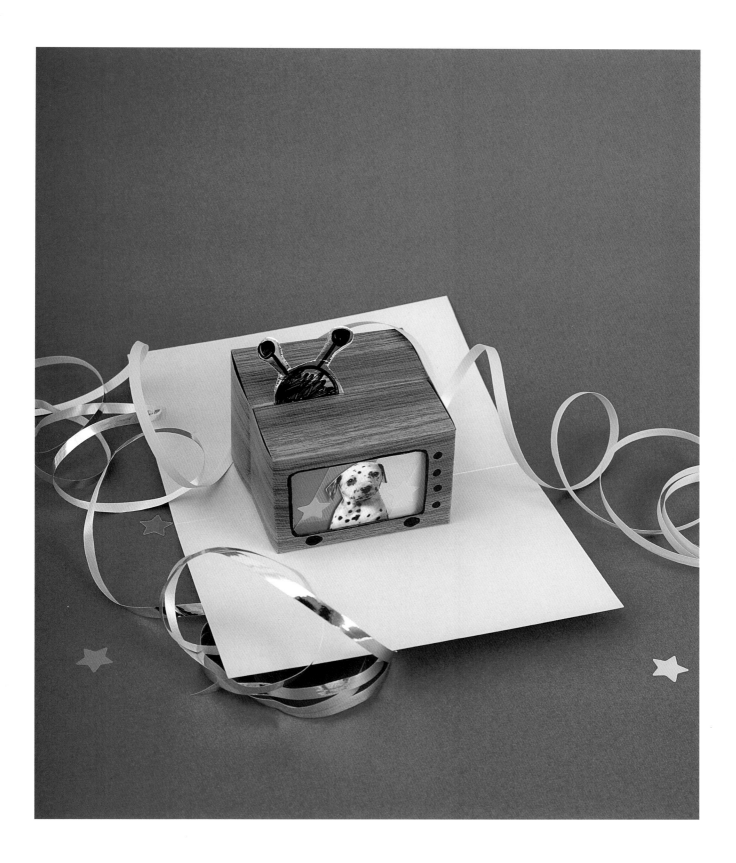

1 Make an A5 (14.8cm x 21cm) card blank from pale green card.

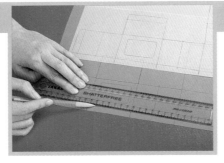

2 Copy the template at the back of the book onto the reverse side of the wood-effect card using tracing paper. Make it 29cm long.

3 Score the lines with a ruler and a knife.

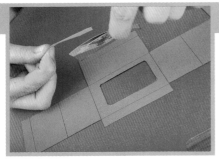

7 Turn the TV over and attach the image you wish to use behind the screen, with tape.

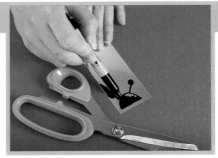

8 Draw an aerial onto silver card with a black marker pen and cut it out.

9 Fold the box inwards along the scored lines.

13 The box will now collapse when the card is closed and pop up when it is opened.

Pop-up Gift Box

The box template can be used to make other pop-up boxes. Try making a pop-up gift box card, using red holographic card and silver holographic tape for the ribbon. Draw the bow with a black marker pen onto a scrap of card covered with the holographic tape. Cut around the edge of the bow and glue it to the central box flap as you did with the aerial on the TV.

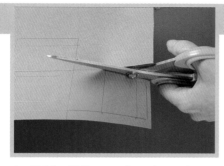

4   Cut the TV box out from the card.

5   Cut out the screen with a craft knife on a cutting mat.

6   Turn over the TV, draw a line around the TV screen with a black marker pen and draw on the knobs.

10   Glue the aerial to the flap in the middle of the TV.

11   With double-sided tape, attach the flaps together to form the box.

12   Attach the bottom flap to the centre of the card. The middle flaps should be positioned just behind the score in the card.

TV Origami Envelopes

You could make envelopes from TV guides. Tear pages out of old Sunday supplement magazines or use the newspaper TV guide. Make a TV address label for the front of the envelope. Use left-over, wood-effect paper to make the TV. Use a white sticky address label as the screen.

Templates

Use the templates for the card projects. A straight line indicates a cut. A dotted line indicates a fold.

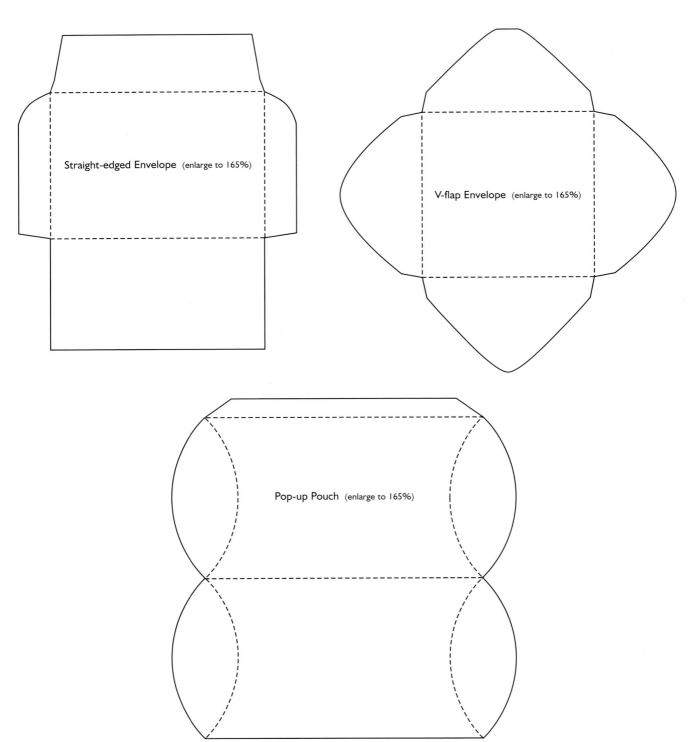

Straight-edged Envelope (enlarge to 165%)

V-flap Envelope (enlarge to 165%)

Pop-up Pouch (enlarge to 165%)

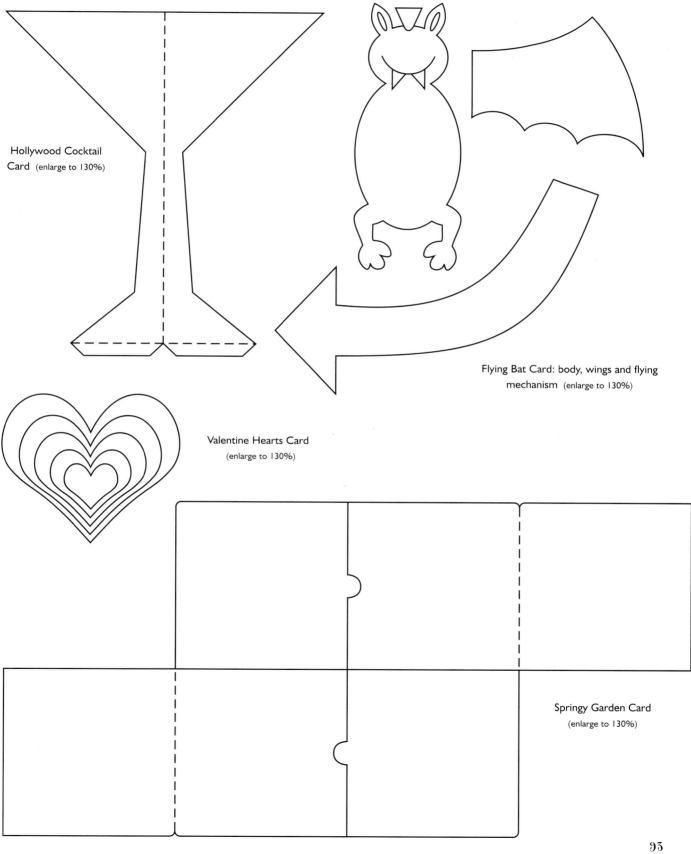

Hollywood Cocktail
Card (enlarge to 130%)

Flying Bat Card: body, wings and flying
mechanism (enlarge to 130%)

Valentine Hearts Card
(enlarge to 130%)

Springy Garden Card
(enlarge to 130%)

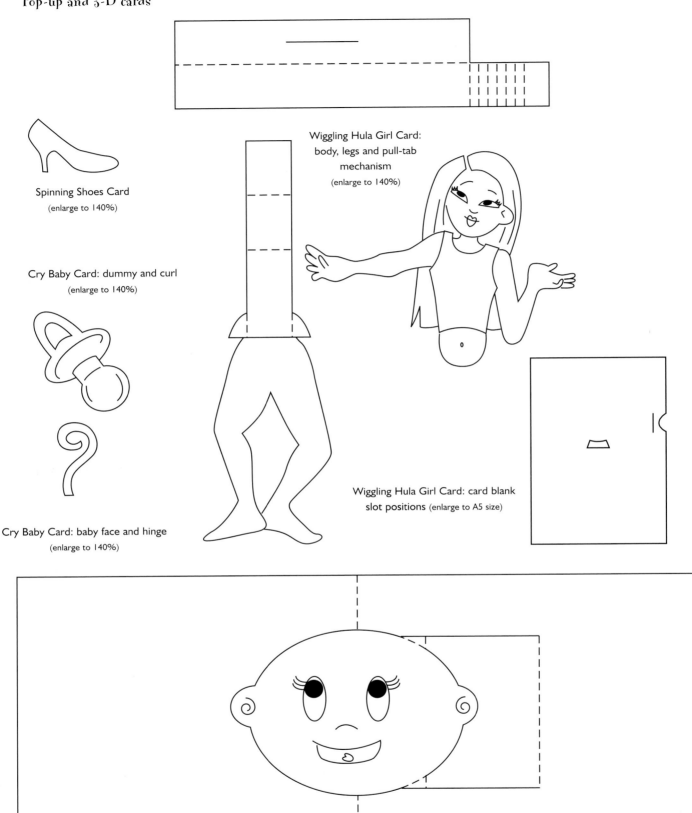

Spinning Shoes Card

(enlarge to 140%)

Cry Baby Card: dummy and curl

(enlarge to 140%)

Wiggling Hula Girl Card:
body, legs and pull-tab
mechanism

(enlarge to 140%)

Cry Baby Card: baby face and hinge

(enlarge to 140%)

Wiggling Hula Girl Card: card blank
slot positions (enlarge to A5 size)

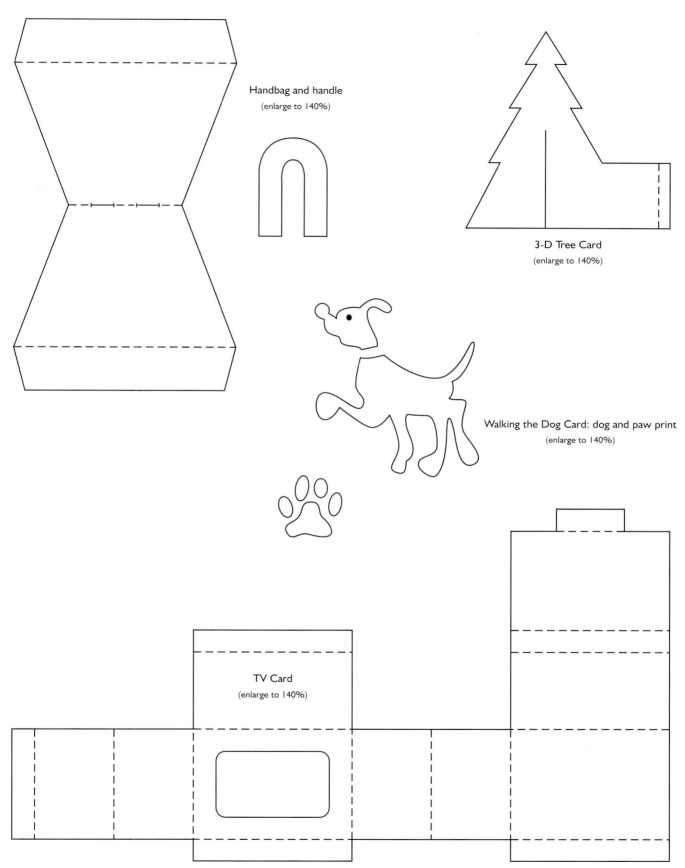

Handbag and handle
(enlarge to 140%)

3-D Tree Card
(enlarge to 140%)

Walking the Dog Card: dog and paw print
(enlarge to 140%)

TV Card
(enlarge to 140%)

Glossary

A-sizes: The standard measurements of paper available internationally. (International paper sizing. ISO standard)

Size	Dimensions	Uses
A0	84.1 x 118.9cm	technical drawings, posters
A1	59.4 x 84.1cm	flip charts
A2	42 x 59.4cm	drawings, diagrams, large tables
A3	29.7 x 42cm	drawings, diagrams
A4	21 x 29.7cm	letters, magazines, forms, laser printers and copying machines
A5	14.8 x 21cm	greeting cards, note pads
A6	10.5 x 14.8cm	postcards

Against the grain: Opposite way to the way fibres are running.

Animated mouth or **beak:** Based upon the V-fold, the paper simulates a talking action, when the card is opened up and closed.

Box cut: Two cuts through the spine of a card. When the card is opened and the cut section pushed through, a box appears.

C-sizes: The standard sizes for envelopes, designed to be used with A-sized paper. The sizes are classified as follows:
A C4 envelope (22.9 x 32.4cm) fits a flat A4 sheet.
A C5 envelope (16.2 x 22.9cm) fits an A4 sheet folded once.
A C6 envelope (11.4 x 16.2cm) fits an A5 sheet folded once.

Card blank: A scored and folded blank piece of card.

Concertina: A series of folds, back and forth that create the same effect as an accordion or concertina.

Crease: Folding along a scored line. (*see also* Score)

Cracking: Folding can damage the paper's fibres and result in cracking. Heavier papers should be scored to create a smooth, straight fold.

Cut lines: Indicated on the templates (at the back of the book) by a continuous line.

Debossing: The opposite of embossing. Instead of a raised image, letters or textures are depressed into a sheet with a metal plate.

Double page pop-up: This is when the pop-up element or illustration lies across two adjacent sides of a card.

DL envelope: An A4 sheet folded twice fits into a DL envelope. It is also known as a Banker because it is large enough to accommodate a flat cheque. A DL envelope is 11cm x 22cm.

Electronic printing: Colour copiers, photocopiers, ink jet and laser printers create images using electrostatic charges or ink sprays. A cheap and effective way of copying and enlarging images. To enlarge images, take this book along to your local print shop.

Embossing: The use of pressure and a metal die to create a raised letter or image on paper.

Fibre: Paper can be described as a thin sheet of pulped fibres. The fibres found in most papers are from wood or reclaimed wood. Cotton and synthetic fibers are sometimes used.

Fluorescent paint: A very colourful, bright paint that reflects light.

Fold: Indicated by a broken line of dashes in the templates at the back of the book.

Fold-cut: A cut in a fold.

Grain: The direction in which most fibers lie in a machine-made sheet of paper. The fibers in handmade paper are random.

Holographic card: Printed smooth card with a 3-D effect or pattern on its surface.

International paper sizing: The International Standards Organisation (ISO) defines a series of paper sizes. The most important of these for daily office use is A4. Books and newspapers use B sizes, while envelopes use C sizes. The US has a different set of standards. (*see* A-sizes and C-sizes)

Laid paper: Laid or textured finish papers feature a subtle texture. Often used for stationery or business cards.

Laminate: Layering and gluing materials together, e.g. cloth on card or two sheets of paper.

Opaque: Able to see through but not fully transparent.

Origami: The Japanese art of folding paper to create a functional or decorative item, without the use of scissors or glue. Specialist origami paper can be bought that allows precise folds and creasing. It is often highly decorative with ornate Japanese designs such as cherry blossoms.

Pull-tabs: Paper extensions from an illustration which when pulled, pushed, or slid cause the illustration to move or pop-up.

Pulp: Pulp is generally made from wood fibres, or reclaimed wood fibres. Pulp can be fine to make smooth paper or left chunky to create lumps and bumps in the paper, such as with handmade paper.

Score: An impression in the paper made by grazing with a knife or pressing with a blunt object such as a knitting needle. This will allow the paper to fold more easily.

Slit: A thin cut made with a craft knife.

Spine: The outside edge of a folded card blank.

Spinning wheel: A disc of paper secured to the back of the card by a split pin. Cut holes in the card allow patterns or illustrations drawn around the wheel to show through the holes.

Springs: Folded or concertinaed paper that will compress and expand.

Thickness: Measured in thousandths of an inch for card and paper.

Triptych: Three-sided card that folds inwards.

Tunnel: A series of cut-out shapes, spaced one behind the other. The overlapping of the various cut-outs creates a sense of depth, like looking into a tunnel.

V-fold: Triangular folds around a slit or crease, which allow movement when the card is opened and folded.

Weight: The weight of paper is measured in grams per square metre (gsm). 170–290 gsm are useful weights of paper for making cards.